easy sushi rolls

and miso soups

easy sushi rolls
and miso soups

Fiona Smith Photography by Diana Miller

RYLAND
PETERS
& SMALL

LONDON NEW YORK

First published in Great Britain in 2004
20–21 Jockey's Fields,
London WC1R 4BW
www.rylandpeters.com

10 9 8 7 6 5 4 3 2

Text © Fiona Smith 2004
Design and photographs
© Ryland Peters & Small 2004

Printed in China

ISBN 1 84172 577 3

A CIP record for this book is available
from the British Library.

Senior Designer Steve Painter
Commissioning Editor
Elsa Petersen-Schepelern
Production Deborah Wehner
Art Director Gabriella Le Grazie
Publishing Director Alison Starling

Food Stylist Lucy McKelvie
Prop Stylist Hélène Lesur

Author's acknowledgements
Thank you so very much to my mother
Naomi and my editor Elsa for all their
help and support.
Thanks also to Lucy McKelvie, Helen
Lesur, Diana Miller and Steve Painter for
making the food look gorgeous.
I am very grateful to Koji Maruura, from
Japan Mart in Auckland, who helped me
so much with advice and ingredients.

Notes
• All spoon measurements are level
unless otherwise specified.
• All eggs are medium unless otherwise
specified. Uncooked or partly cooked
eggs should not be served to the very
young, the very old, those with
compromised immune systems or
to pregnant women.
• Japanese ingredients are now widely
available in larger supermarkets, health
food stores and Asian markets.

contents

serving sushi rolls

Sushi has come a long way in a relatively short time. It always amazes me to think how the mystique surrounding this style of food kept it from being a favourite with home cooks for so long.

But how things have changed! Fresh sushi can be found everywhere from restaurants to supermarkets and fast-food outlets. It is served at elegant parties or the simplest home gatherings. Travel-weary tourists choose sushi restaurants for comforting, familiar food. Children have it in their lunchboxes, and even some school canteens serve it. Sushi has become this generation's healthy convenience food.

Techniques used in making sushi can be simplified for the home cook. One of the most popular styles, rolled sushi (*maki-zushi*) is easy and fun to make at home and, as soon as the process of rolling the rice has been mastered, a world of filling options becomes available. These days, our supermarkets are full of all kinds of sushi ingredients.

Sushi-making utensils and ingredients

Special sushi-making utensils and authentic ingredients are beautiful and useful, and sold even in supermarkets. Many brands of nori are available pretoasted and in a variety of grades—use the best you can.

Some of the recipes in this book call for only half a sheet. When this is so, cut the sheets in half from the shortest side, so you are left with the most width. When making rolled sushi remember that rice is easier to handle with wet hands and nori is better to handle with dry. Keep a bowl of vinegared water and a towel on hand to make the job easier.

Serving sushi

Traditional accompaniments for sushi are soy sauce, wasabi paste and pickled ginger, and it is often served with miso soup. A smear of wasabi can elevate a piece of sushi from the ordinary to something extraordinary. I have indicated when I think wasabi is important in a recipe. If you do not want to add it in the sushi, serve a small mound on the side, or serve the sushi with a small dish of plain soy and one of wasabi and soy mixed together. Bought wasabi varies immensely; it is possible to find paste with a high percentage of real wasabi, but many are mostly horseradish—once again, buy the best you can or make your own (page 62).

Sushi is traditionally served immediately, but if you have to keep it for a while, wrap uncut rolls in plastic wrap. Keep in a cool place, but NOT in the refrigerator, which will make the rice hard and unpleasant—the vinegar in the rice will help preserve it for a short time.

cooking rice

The key to making sushi is the rice – vinegared rice, or *sumeshi*. Proper Japanese sushi rice is widely available now, so there is no need to compromise. It has a slightly rounder grain and is stickier than regular long grain rice, so it will hold together better. Never put cooked sushi rice in the refrigerator – it will become hard and unpleasant. Instead, keep it covered in a cool place. The vinegar will help to preserve it.

seasoned sushi rice

325 g sushi rice (short grain)*
5 cm strip of kombu (dried kelp)*

vinegared seasoning

3 tablespoons rice vinegar
4 teaspoons caster sugar
½ teaspoon salt

makes 1 litre

Various kinds of dried seaweed, such as kombu, nori and wakame, as well as sushi rice and sushi-making equipment, are available in larger supermarkets, health food stores and Japanese shops.

To make the vinegared seasoning, put the rice vinegar, sugar and salt in a small bowl and stir until dissolved. (Doing this first gives it time to dissolve.)

Put the rice in a colander and wash under cold running water, shaking the rice around to ensure it is washed well. Let drain for 30 minutes (this starts the grains absorbing water).

Transfer the rice to a medium saucepan, add the kombu and cover with 350 ml water. Bring to the boil, stirring, then reduce to a very low simmer. Cover and cook without stirring for 10 minutes. Remove from the heat and set aside, covered, for 10 minutes.

Transfer the rice to a large, non-metal bowl – traditionally a flat wooden tub called a *hangiri* – and remove the kombu. Pour the vinegared seasoning over the rice and, using a wooden rice paddle or wooden spoon, cut the seasoning through the rice, cutting and turning the rice for about 2 minutes. Take care not to mash the grains (you will feel it become stickier as you turn it).

Cover the rice with a damp cloth and let cool to room temperature before using. Do not refrigerate.

Futo-maki (thick rolled) sushi are great for lunch, because they are more substantial than *hosi-maki* (thin rolled). However, they aren't ideal for fingerfood, because they are more than one mouthful.

five-colour roll

10 g dry gourd*

2 teaspoons salt, for rubbing

250 ml dashi or fish stock

2 teaspoons Japanese soy sauce

2 teaspoons mirin (sweetened Japanese rice wine)

1 teaspoon sugar

3 eggs

a pinch of salt

2 teaspoons peanut oil

150 g spinach leaves, washed

3 sheets of nori

½ recipe seasoned sushi rice (page 9)

1 small red pepper, halved, deseeded and cut into fine strips

1 medium carrot, grated or very thinly sliced

a 28 cm frying pan

makes 24

*Gourd (kampyo or calabash) is sold dried in Japanese shops. It is a common ingredient in rolled sushi, and worth trying.

Fill a bowl with water, add the gourd, rub the salt into the gourd to wash it, then drain and rinse thoroughly. Cover the gourd with fresh water and soak for 1 hour. Drain, then put in a saucepan, cover with boiling water and cook for 5 minutes. Drain, return to the pan, then add the dashi, 1 teaspoon of the soy, 1 teaspoon of the mirin and the sugar. Bring to the boil, reduce the heat and simmer for 5 minutes. Let cool in the liquid, then drain.

Put the eggs in a bowl, add the salt and remaining soy and mirin, and mix well. Heat the oil in the frying pan over medium heat. Pour in the eggs, swirling the pan so the mixture covers the base. Cook for 2–3 minutes, gently gathering in the cooked omelette around the edges to let the uncooked egg run onto the hot pan. When the egg is set, take off the heat and fold in the 4 sides, so they meet in the middle and the omelette is now double thickness and square. Remove to a board, let cool, then slice into 3 strips.

Wipe out and reheat the pan. Add the washed but still wet spinach and cover. Cook for 1½–2 minutes until wilted. Tip into a colander and let cool for a few minutes. Using your hands, squeeze out the liquid from the spinach.

Put 1 nori sheet on a rolling mat, rough side up, and spread with one-third of the rice, leaving 3 cm nori bare at the far edge. Put a strip of omelette in the middle and put one-third of the gourd, spinach, pepper and carrot, laid in lengthways strips on top.

Carefully roll up the nori in the mat, pressing the ingredients into the roll as you go. Wet the bare edge of nori and finish rolling to seal. Repeat to make 3 rolls, then cut each one into 8 pieces.

vegetarian

A thinly sliced ribbon of courgette makes a stunning alternative to nori on the outside of a sushi roll. It is easiest to cut the courgette and beetroot using a mandoline – the plastic Japanese ones are marvellous – but if you don't have one you can use a good sharp peeler or a sharp knife and a steady hand.

pickled courgette roll
with beetroot sashimi

250 ml rice vinegar

60 g sugar

2 tablespoons mirin (sweetened Japanese rice wine)

3 medium courgettes (green or yellow, or both)

1–2 very small beetroot or 5–6 baby beetroot, uncooked

1 teaspoon wasabi paste

1½ tablespoons Japanese mayonnaise

½ recipe seasoned sushi rice (page 9)

dipping sauce

2 tablespoons Japanese mild soy sauce

1 tablespoon sake

makes 18

To make the pickling mixture, put the vinegar, sugar and mirin in a small saucepan and bring to the boil, stirring. Reduce to a simmer and cook for 5 minutes. Remove from the heat and let cool.

Thinly slice the courgettes lengthways, discarding the first and last couple of pieces (they will be too narrow). Arrange the slices flat in a shallow dish or container and pour the pickling mixture over the top. Set aside for 4 hours or overnight.

When ready to assemble the sushi, peel the raw beetroot and slice carefully, as thinly as possible.

Put the wasabi and mayonnaise in a small bowl and mix well.

Divide the seasoned rice into 18 portions about the size of a walnut, and shape each piece into a flattened ball. Wrap a ribbon of pickled courgette around the outside of each piece, top with a dab of wasabi mayonnaise and thin slivers of raw beetroot.

To make the dipping sauce, mix the soy sauce and sake together and serve in a small bowl beside the sushi.

One simple ingredient can make a perfectly elegant filling for rolled sushi. Here fresh green asparagus is marinated in white miso.

miso marinated asparagus roll

24 small or 12 medium
asparagus spears

100 g white miso paste

2 teaspoons mirin (sweetened
Japanese rice wine)

1 teaspoon wasabi paste

3 sheets of nori, halved

½ recipe seasoned sushi rice
(page 9)

makes 36

Snap off any tough ends of the asparagus and discard. Bring a large saucepan of water to the boil, add the asparagus and simmer for 3–4 minutes until tender. Drain, rinse in plenty of cold water, then let cool.

If using medium asparagus, slice each piece in half lengthways to give 24 pieces in total. Arrange all the asparagus in a shallow dish.

Put the white miso paste, mirin and wasabi paste in a small bowl and mix well. Spread evenly over the asparagus and let marinate for 2–4 hours.

When ready to assemble the rolls, carefully scrape the marinade off the asparagus – it should be fairly clean, so the miso doesn't overwhelm the flavour.

Put 1 half-sheet of nori, rough side up, on a rolling mat, a piece of clingfilm or a tea towel. The long edge of the nori sheet should be towards you. Divide the rice into 6 portions. Spread 1 portion in a thin layer on the nori, leaving about 2 cm bare on the far edge.

Put 4 pieces of the asparagus in a line along the middle of the rice. Lift the edge of the mat closest to you and start rolling up the sushi away from you, pressing in the filling with your fingers as you roll. You may need a little water along the far edge to seal it. Repeat to make 6 rolls in all.

Using a clean, wet knife, slice each roll into 6 even pieces and serve.

Rolling inside-out sushi may seem a bit tricky, but it is actually very easy, because the rice on the outside moulds so well into shape, and it has the added bonus of looking spectacular.

inside-out avocado rolls
with chives and cashews

2 small or 1 large ripe avocado

2 teaspoons lemon juice

2 tablespoons Japanese mayonnaise

¼ teaspoon salt

1 teaspoon wasabi paste (optional)

75 g cashew nuts, toasted (roasted, salted cashews work well)

a small bunch of chives

2 sheets of nori, halved

½ recipe seasoned sushi rice (page 9)

makes 24

Peel the avocado and cut the flesh into small chunks. Toss in a bowl with the lemon juice, mayonnaise, salt and wasabi, if using. Mash slightly as you toss but not until mushy! Divide into 4 portions.

Chop the cashew nuts very finely and put in a bowl. Chop the chives very finely and mix with the cashew nuts. Divide into 4 portions.

Put a sheet of clingfilm on the rolling mat. Put ½ sheet nori on top, rough side up, with the long edge facing you. Divide the rice into 4 portions and spread 1 portion over the nori.

Sprinkle 1 portion of the nut and chive mixture on top of the rice. Press it in gently with your fingers.

Carefully lift the whole thing up and flip it over so the rice is face down on the clingfilm. Remove the sushi mat. Put 1 portion of the avocado in a line along the long edge of the nori closest to you. Carefully roll it up, then cut in half, then each half into 3, giving 6 pieces. Repeat to make 4 rolls, giving 24 pieces.

Mushrooms are a popular Japanese vegetable. Many of our regular supermarkets carry fresh shiitakes, and also may have enokis, like little clumps of white nails with tiny caps, and their bigger brothers, the hon-shigiri, with brown 'berets' on their heads. If unavailable, use oyster and button mushrooms.

mushroom omelette sushi roll

100 g fresh shiitake mushrooms, about 12, stalks removed

100 g oyster mushrooms

50 g enoki mushrooms, roots trimmed

3 teaspoons peanut oil

1 tablespoon Japanese soy sauce

1 tablespoon mirin (sweetened Japanese rice wine)

2 eggs

¼ teaspoon salt

½ recipe seasoned sushi rice (page 9)

4 sheets of nori

a 23 cm frying pan, preferably non-stick

makes 24–32

Slice the shiitake and oyster mushrooms into 1 cm slices. Separate the enoki mushrooms into bunches of two or three.

Heat 2 teaspoons of the oil in a large frying pan and sauté the shiitake and oyster mushrooms for 2 minutes, add the enoki and stir-fry for 1½ minutes. Add the soy sauce and mirin and toss to coat. Remove from the heat and let cool. Divide into 4 portions.

Put the eggs and salt in a bowl and beat well. Heat ½ teaspoon of the oil in a frying pan. Slowly pour in half of the egg, tipping the pan to get an even coating. Cook for about 1 minute until set, roll up, remove from the pan and let cool. Repeat with the remaining egg to make a second omelette. Slice the two rolled omelettes in half lengthways.

Divide the rice into 4 portions. Put 1 nori sheet on a rolling mat, rough side up, and spread with 1 portion of rice, leaving 3 cm of bare nori at the far edge. Put a strip of omelette down the middle and top with 1 portion of the mushrooms. Carefully roll up the nori in the mat, pressing the ingredients into the roll as you go. Wet the bare edge of nori and finish rolling to seal. Repeat to make 4 rolls.

Slice each roll into 6–8 pieces and serve.

**Silken tofu makes a moist, tender filling –
I think that firm tofu can be a bit tough. To
make silken tofu a little firmer, put it in a
bowl and cover it with boiling water before
you start making the sushi.**

grilled tofu roll

175 g silken tofu

2 tablespoons Japanese soy sauce

1 tablespoon mirin (sweetened Japanese rice wine)

1 teaspoon sugar

3 sheets of nori, halved (you need 5 pieces, so you will have ½ sheet left over)

1 tablespoon white sesame seeds, toasted in a dry frying pan

1 tablespoon black sesame seeds

1 tablespoon oboro (dried pink fish flakes)

½ recipe seasoned sushi rice (page 9)

1 teaspoon wasabi paste

a metal tray, lined with baking parchment

makes 24–32

Cut the tofu into 1 cm square strips and arrange in a shallow dish. Put the soy sauce, mirin and sugar in a small bowl or jug and mix well. Pour the mixture evenly over the tofu and set aside to marinate for 10 minutes.

Preheat the grill. Place the tofu on a metal tray lined with baking parchment and grill for 2 minutes, turn the pieces over, brush with marinade and grill for a further 2 minutes. Set aside to cool.

Cut ½ sheet of nori into tiny shreds (about 3 mm), put in a small bowl and stir in the white and black sesame seeds and oboro.

Divide the rice into 4 portions.

Spread a sheet of clingfilm on top of the rolling mat. Put ½ sheet of nori on this and spread with 1 portion of rice. Sprinkle with a quarter of the seed mixture, and press lightly into the rice.

Carefully lift the whole thing up and flip it over so the rice is face down on the clingfilm. Arrange slices of grilled tofu along the long edge of the nori closest to you, smear with a little wasabi paste and carefully roll up. Repeat to make 4 rolls, then slice each roll into 6–8 pieces.

Serve with extra wasabi and your choice of accompaniments.

This simple little roll makes a colourful addition to a sushi board. Try using a selection of different vegetables such as carrot, cucumber, radish, beetroot, and red, yellow or orange peppers.

bright vegetable and thin omelette rolls

3 large eggs

2 teaspoons Japanese soy sauce

2–3 teaspoons peanut oil

½ recipe seasoned sushi rice (page 9)

3 sheets of nori, halved

100 g mixed vegetables (see recipe introduction), shredded into fine matchsticks

1 teaspoon wasabi paste (optional)

a Japanese omelette pan or 20 cm frying pan

makes 36

Put the eggs and soy sauce in a jug or bowl and beat well. Heat a film of oil in the pan and pour in one-third of the beaten egg mixture. Swirl the egg around to cover the base of the pan and cook for about 1 minute until set. Carefully remove the omelette to a plate and cook the remaining egg mixture in 2 batches. Cut each omelette in half.

Divide the rice into 6 portions.

Put a sheet of nori on a rolling mat with the long edge towards you, rough side up. Top with 1 portion of the rice and piece of omelette (trim the end of the omelette if it hangs over the end of the rice). Arrange a line of vegetables along the edge closest to you and smear a little wasabi, if using, in a line next to the vegetables.

Carefully roll up, brushing a little water along the edge of the nori to seal if necessary. Repeat to make 6 rolls, then slice each roll into 6 even pieces.

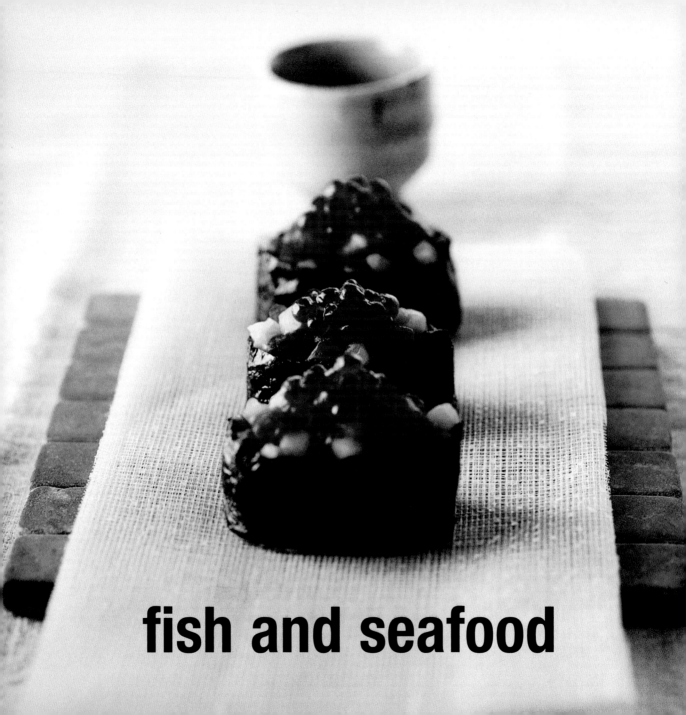

fish and seafood

Battleship sushi is individually hand rolled so the nori comes about half a centimetre above the rice, leaving room for less manageable toppings such as fish roe. Small cubes of different-coloured fish make a lovely topping and you don't need to be an expert fish slicer to get tender pieces. You do, however, need very fresh raw fish – that is what 'sushi- or sashimi-grade' means. If you have access to a proper Japanese fishmonger, that's perfect. Otherwise, go to a fish market, or other outlet where you can be sure the fish is ultra-fresh.

treasures of the sea
battleship sushi

75 g piece of sushi-grade raw salmon

75 g piece of sushi-grade raw tuna

75 g piece of sushi-grade raw white fish (try sea bream or halibut)

½ recipe seasoned sushi rice (page 9)

4 sheets of nori

1 teaspoon wasabi paste (optional)

1 tablespoon salmon caviar (keta)

makes 18

Cut the salmon, tuna and white fish into ½ centimetre cubes, put in a bowl and mix gently.

Divide the seasoned sushi rice into 18 portions, a little smaller than a table tennis ball. Gently squeeze each piece into a flattened oval shape, about 2 cm high. With dry hands, cut the nori sheets into 2.5 cm strips, and wrap each piece of rice in one strip with the rough side of the nori facing inwards. Seal the ends with a dab of water. You should have about ½ centimetre of nori above the rice.

Put a dab of wasabi, if using, on top of the rice, then add a heaped teaspoon of the fish cubes, and a little salmon caviar.

This larger hand roll is still small enough to be held and eaten easily, but also makes a great starter or lunch if you allow 3 rolls per person. Choose any smoked fish, but make sure it is moist and soft.

smoked fish hand roll

1 small red onion, finely sliced

1 tablespoon rice vinegar

180 g smoked fish, such as trout, salmon or eel

5 cm piece of cucumber

6 sheets of nori, about 21 x 18 cm

½ recipe seasoned sushi rice (page 9)

1 teaspoon wasabi paste (optional)

1 small carrot, finely sliced into thin strips

1 small red pepper, finely sliced into thin strips

makes 18

Put the onion in a small saucepan with the vinegar and 4 tablespoons water. Bring to the boil, drain and let cool.

Cut the smoked fish into even strips, about 6 x 1 cm long – you should have 18 even pieces.

Quarter the cucumber lengthways, scrape out the seeds, then cut into fine strips.

Cut each sheet of nori into 3 pieces (7 x 18 cm).

Put a piece of nori on a work surface with the long edge towards you and the rough side up. Spread 1 small heaped teaspoon of rice crossways over the nori about a quarter of the way in from the left edge. Smear with a little wasabi, if using. Top the rice with a piece of fish, a few strips of carrot, red pepper and cucumber and a little red onion, pressing slightly into the rice to hold it firm while you roll.

Take the bottom left corner of the nori and fold it diagonally so the left edge meets the top edge. Continue folding the whole triangle. Arrange with the join downwards on a serving plate or tray. Repeat to make 18 rolls altogether.

Oboro are fine white fish flakes, usually coloured pink, making them perfect for adding a splash of colour to sushi. These tiny hand rolls are very easy to eat with your fingers, and so make perfect party food. If you mix all the ingredients before rolling the sushi, the process will be a lot easier.

california roll

7 cm piece of cucumber

150 g crabmeat

1 small or ½ medium (firm) avocado, cut into small cubes

½ recipe seasoned sushi rice (page 9)

6–7 sheets of nori

1 teaspoon wasabi paste (optional)

1 tablespoon oboro (optional, see recipe introduction)

makes 60–70

Slice the cucumber in half lengthways and scrape out the seeds. Chop the flesh into tiny cubes and put in a bowl. Add the crabmeat, avocado and rice and mix gently.

Cut each sheet of nori in half lengthways, then cut the halves into 5 pieces crossways (9 x 4 cm).

Put 1 piece of nori on a work surface with the long edge towards you and the rough side up. Spread 1 teaspoon of the rice mixture crossways over the nori about quarter of the way in from the left edge. Smear the rice with a little wasabi, if using. Take the bottom left corner of the nori and fold it diagonally so the left edge meets the top edge, then continue folding the whole triangle. Sprinkle the open end with a little oboro, if using. Repeat until all the ingredients have been used.

The crunch of tempura batter is delicious in sushi, although the batter will soften as it cools. If you have some left-over batter, use it to cook a few of your favourite vegetables or for the tempura croutons for miso soup on page 58.

tempura prawn roll

24 large uncooked prawns, peeled, but with tail fins intact

2 sheets of nori

½ recipe seasoned sushi rice (page 9)

1 teaspoon wasabi (optional)

25 g mizuna or baby spinach

peanut or sunflower oil, for frying

tempura batter

1 egg, separated

1 tablespoon lemon juice

150 ml iced water

60 g plain flour

24 bamboo skewers

makes 24

Fill a large wok or saucepan one-third full with oil and heat to 190°C (375°F), or until a small cube of bread turns golden in 30 seconds.

Thread each prawn onto a skewer to straighten it for cooking.

To make the batter, put the egg yolk, lemon juice and iced water in a bowl. Whisk gently, then whisk in the flour to form a smooth batter. Do not overmix.

Whisk the egg white in a second bowl until stiff but not dry, then fold into the batter.

Dip each prawn into the batter and fry for 1–2 minutes until crisp and golden. Drain on crumpled kitchen paper and let cool for 5 minutes. Remove the skewers.

With dry hands, cut the nori sheets in half crossways and then into 3 cm strips. Spread 1 tablespoon of rice over each piece of nori, top with a tempura prawn, a dab of wasabi, if using, and a little mizuna or baby spinach. Roll up to secure the filling. Brush the nori with water to help it stick, if necessary. Repeat until all the ingredients have been used.

Squid is delicious in sushi, but can be tricky when raw, because it does tend to be tough. If you braise it slowly, you end up with deliciously tender pieces.

slow-cooked squid

250 g baby squid bodies, 8 cm long (about 12), cleaned

1 teaspoon mirin (sweetened Japanese rice wine)

1 teaspoon soy sauce

½ teaspoon finely chopped fresh red chilli

½ teaspoon finely chopped garlic

1 teaspoon grated fresh ginger

1 tablespoon finely chopped fresh coriander

½ recipe seasoned sushi rice (page 9)

1 tablespoon black sesame seeds

an oven tray or grill tray

makes 24

Slice the squid bodies in half lengthways and arrange on an oven tray or grill tray. Sprinkle with the mirin and soy. Set the tray at least 15 cm away from a preheated grill so the heat is not too fierce. Grill for about 8 minutes or until the squid turns opaque. Remove and let cool.

Put the squid in a bowl, add the chilli, garlic, ginger and coriander, stir gently, cover and let marinate in the refrigerator for 1 hour.

Divide the rice into 24 balls about the size of a small walnut. Top each rice ball with a piece of squid using the natural curl of the squid body to hold it securely. Sprinkle each with a few black sesame seeds, then serve.

Yakitori is the name given to food grilled on skewers over a charcoal fire. It can be anything – chicken, steak, liver, or the octopus used here. Prawns, scallops or any firm fish also work well. You should cook the octopus very fast over a fire to get an authentic flavour, but a hot grill will also work.

yakitori octopus roll

6 octopus tentacles, about 1 kg, tenderized, skin and suckers removed

6 spring onions

2 tablespoons sake

2 tablespoons Japanese soy sauce

1 teaspoon sugar

1 teaspoon freshly grated ginger

3 sheets of nori, halved

½ recipe seasoned sushi rice (page 9), divided into 6 portions

5 bamboo skewers, soaked in water for 30 minutes

makes 30

Cut the octopus into 2-cm pieces. Cut the spring onions into 2-cm lengths. Thread the pieces of octopus and spring onion alternately crossways onto the soaked skewers.

Put the sake, soy, sugar and ginger into a small bowl or jug, mix well, then pour over the octopus skewers and let marinate at room temperature for 30 minutes, turning occasionally.

Preheat a barbecue or grill to very hot. Set the yakitori skewers about 7 cm from the heat and cook for 4–5 minutes, turning once. Remove from the heat and let cool.

Put a sheet of nori, rough side up, on a rolling mat, a piece of clingfilm or a tea towel, with the long edge towards you. Top with 1 portion of the sushi rice, spread in a thin layer, leaving about 2 cm of bare nori on the far edge. Arrange pieces of the octopus, end to end, in a line along the middle of the rice, then put a line of spring onions on top.

Lift the edge of the mat closest to you and start rolling up the sushi away from you, pressing in the filling with your fingers as you roll. You may need a little water along the far edge to seal it. Repeat to make 6 rolls. Using a clean wet knife, slice each roll into 5 even pieces.

Note If the octopus has not been pre-tenderized, you can either beat it with a meat mallet or try this Portuguese method. Wash well and put in a large saucepan with 1 sliced onion. Cover with a lid and slowly bring to the boil over low heat (there will be enough moisture in the octopus to do this without added water). Let simmer for 30–40 minutes until tender. Cool, then pull off and discard the purple skin and suckers.

To many sushi fans, delicious raw fish is part of the pleasure of this dish. However, if you're not an aficionado of fish *au naturel*, using smoked or pickled fish is a delicious compromise. It is very easy to pickle fish at home, and you can control the sharpness more easily.

pickled salmon roll

3 sheets of nori, halved

½ recipe seasoned sushi rice (page 9), divided into 6 portions

1 teaspoon wasabi paste (optional)

pickled salmon

100 ml rice wine vinegar

2 teaspoons salt

2 tablespoons sugar

zest of 1 unwaxed lemon, removed with a lemon zester

300 g salmon fillet, skinned and boned

4 shallots, finely sliced

makes 36–42

To prepare the salmon, put the vinegar, salt, sugar and lemon zest in a saucepan with 60 ml water. Bring to the boil, reduce the heat, then simmer for 3 minutes. Let cool.

Put the salmon fillet in a plastic container with the shallots. Pour the vinegar mixture over the top and cover tightly. Refrigerate for 2–3 days, turning the salmon in the pickle once a day.

When ready to make the sushi, drain the salmon and shallots. Slice the salmon as finely as possible and divide into 6 portions.

Put a half sheet of nori, rough side up, on a rolling mat, a piece of clingfilm or a tea towel, with the long edge towards you. Top with 1 portion of the sushi rice and spread it out in a thin layer, leaving about 2 cm of bare nori at the far edge. Smear a little wasabi down the centre of the rice if you like. Arrange 1 portion of the salmon slices in a line along the middle of the rice and top with a line of the pickled shallots.

Lift the edge of the mat closest to you and start rolling the sushi away from you, pressing in the filling with your fingers as you roll. You may need a little water along the far edge to seal it. Repeat with the remaining ingredients to make 6 rolls. Using a clean wet knife, slice each roll into 6–7 even pieces, then serve.

A fresh uncooked oyster makes an elegantly simple topping for sushi. Chose small oysters if possible – large ones will swamp a delicate roll.

fresh oyster roll
with chilli cucumber

2 sheets of nori

½ recipe seasoned sushi rice (page 9)

freshly squeezed juice of 1 lemon

20 fresh small oysters, shucked

chilli cucumber

125 ml white rice vinegar

2 tablespoons sugar

1 tablespoon mirin (sweetened Japanese rice wine)

7 cm piece cucumber, halved, deseeded and cut into fine matchsticks

2 mild red chillies, halved, deseeded and finely sliced

makes 20

To make the chilli cucumber, put the vinegar, sugar and mirin in a small saucepan and bring to the boil, stirring. Reduce the heat and simmer for 3 minutes. Remove from the heat and let cool.

Put the cucumber and chillies in a plastic bowl and pour over the cooled vinegar mixture. Cover and refrigerate for 24 hours.

When ready to assemble the rolls, put a sheet of nori, rough side up, on a rolling mat, a piece of clingfilm or a tea towel, with the long edge towards you. Add half of the sushi rice and spread it out in a thin layer, leaving about 2 cm of bare nori on the far edge. Lift the edge of the mat closest to you and start rolling the sushi away from you. You may need a little water along the far edge to seal it. Press the roll into an oval. Repeat with the remaining ingredients to make a second roll. Using a clean, wet knife, slice each roll in half, then each half into 5 even pieces, making 20 in all.

Sprinkle lemon juice over the oysters. Top each piece of sushi with an oyster and a little chilli cucumber.

Soaking in vinegar is a way of mellowing the strong flavours of some fish, such as mackerel. If you don't have time to prepare fresh mackerel, try making this sushi with smoked mackerel or other smoked fish for a different, but still delicious flavour.

vinegared mackerel and avocado roll

400 g fresh mackerel fillets (about 2 medium fillets)

2 tablespoons salt

5 tablespoons rice vinegar

1 tablespoon sugar

1 avocado

3 sheets of nori, halved

½ recipe seasoned sushi rice (page 9), divided into 6 portions

1 teaspoon wasabi paste (optional)

makes 36–42

Put the mackerel fillets in a shallow, non-metal bowl and sprinkle on both sides with the salt. Cover with clingfilm and refrigerate for 8 hours or overnight.

Remove the fish from the refrigerator, rinse in cold running water and pat dry with kitchen paper. Put the vinegar and sugar in a shallow dish, mix well, then add the mackerel, turning to coat. Let marinate for 40 minutes at room temperature.

Remove the fish from the marinade and slice diagonally into 1 cm strips. Slice the avocado into 1 cm strips.

Put a sheet of nori, rough side up, on a rolling mat, a piece of clingfilm or a tea towel, with the long edge towards you. Top with 1 portion of the sushi rice and spread it out in a thin layer, leaving about 2 cm of bare nori on the far edge. Smear a little wasabi, if using, down the middle of the rice. Arrange a line of mackerel slices over the wasabi and top with a line of the avocado.

Lift the edge of the mat closest to you and start rolling the sushi away from you, pressing in the filling with your fingers as you roll. You may need a little water along the far edge to seal it. Repeat with the remaining ingredients to make 6 rolls. Using a clean, wet knife, slice each roll into 6–7 even pieces.

Fresh tuna is one of the most popular fillings for sushi. There are three main cuts of tuna, the pink otoro (the finest), chutoro and the dark red akami. With their incredible popularity and high price tags, otoro and chutoro are delicacies reserved for sashimi, but the akami is perfect for rolled sushi.

spicy tuna roll

300 g fresh tuna

2 tablespoons Japanese soy sauce

1 tablespoon sake

1 teaspoon Chinese hot pepper sauce, or chilli sauce

2 spring onions, finely chopped

3 sheets of nori, halved

½ recipe seasoned sushi rice (page 9), divided into 6 portions

makes 36–42 pieces

Slice the tuna into 1 cm strips and put in a shallow dish. Mix the soy sauce, sake, hot pepper sauce and spring onions in a bowl. Pour over the tuna and stir well to coat. Cover and let marinate for 30 minutes. Divide into 6 portions.

Put ½ sheet of nori, rough side up, on a rolling mat, with the long edge towards you. Top with 1 portion of the sushi rice and spread in a thin layer, leaving about 2 cm of bare nori on the far edge. Set one-sixth of the tuna strips in a line along the middle of the rice.

Lift the edge of the mat closest to you and start rolling up the sushi away from you, pressing in the filling with your fingers as you roll. You may need a little water along the far edge to seal it. Repeat to make 6 rolls. Using a clean wet knife, slice each roll into 6–7 even pieces.

This is a very Western idea of sushi, but I have it on good authority that it is acceptable, and also easy and convenient because it uses canned tuna. Use Japanese mayonnaise if you can, but homemade or good-quality bought mayonnaise works well.

wasabi mayonnaise and tuna roll

4 sheets of nori

185 g canned tuna in brine, drained

4 teaspoons Japanese or other mayonnaise

1 teaspoon wasabi paste, or to taste

125 g baby corn, fresh or frozen, or equivalent drained canned baby corn

½ recipe seasoned sushi rice (page 9), divided into 4 portions

makes 24–28 pieces

Trim 2½ cm strip from one long edge of each sheet of nori and reserve for another use.

Put the tuna and mayonnaise in a bowl and stir in the wasabi.

If using fresh or frozen corn, bring a saucepan of water to the boil, and cook the corn for 3 minutes, or until tender. Drain and rinse under cold water to cool. If using canned corn, drain and rinse.

Set a sheet of nori, rough side up, on a rolling mat, a piece of clingfilm or tea towel, with the long edge towards you. Top with 1 portion of the sushi rice, and spread it in a thin layer, leaving about 2 cm of bare nori on the far edge. Spoon one-quarter of the tuna mixture in a line along the middle of the rice and top with a line of corn, set end to end.

Lift the edge of the mat closest to you and start rolling up the sushi away from you, pressing in the filling with your fingers as you roll. You may need a little water along the far edge to seal it. Repeat to make 4 rolls. Using a clean, wet knife, slice each roll into 6–7 even pieces.

teriyaki chicken roll

with miso dipping sauce

400 g boneless, skinless chicken thigh or breast (2 breasts, 4 thighs), cut into 1 cm strips

4 sheets of nori

½ recipe seasoned sushi rice (page 9) divided into 4 portions

1 teaspoon wasabi paste

teriyaki sauce

2 tablespoons Japanese soy sauce

2 tablespoons mirin (sweetened Japanese rice wine)

2 tablespoons chicken stock

teriyaki glaze

1 teaspoon sugar

½ teaspoon cornflour

miso dipping sauce

2 tablespoons white miso paste

1 tablespoon sugar

125 ml sake

1 small egg yolk

12 bamboo skewers soaked in water for 30 minutes

makes 24–28

To make the teriyaki sauce, mix the soy, mirin and chicken stock in a small saucepan and bring to the boil. Remove from the heat and let cool.

To make the teriyaki glaze, mix the sugar and cornflour in a small bowl with a little cold water to slacken, then stir in 2 tablespoons of the teriyaki sauce. Set aside.

Thread the strips of chicken onto the soaked skewers. Brush the chicken skewers with half the teriyaki sauce and let marinate for about 10 minutes. Preheat a grill or barbecue to very hot. Set the chicken skewers under or over the grill. Grill for 2–3 minutes, turn the skewers over and brush with more sauce and grill for a further 2–3 minutes until cooked. Remove from the heat, pour over the teriyaki glaze, let cool, then unthread. The chicken must be cold.

Set a sheet of nori, rough side up, on a rolling mat, piece of clingfilm or tea towel, with the long edge towards you. Top with quarter of the sushi rice, spread in a thin layer covering about half of the nori closest to you. Put a quarter of the chicken in a line along the middle of the rice and smear with a little wasabi.

Lift the edge of the mat closest to you and start rolling up the sushi away from you, pressing in the filling with your fingers as you roll. You may need a little water along the far edge to seal it. Repeat with the remaining ingredients, to make 4 rolls. Using a clean wet knife, slice each roll into 6–7 even pieces.

To make the white miso dipping sauce, put the miso, sugar and sake in a small saucepan over medium heat and bring to a simmer, reduce the heat to low, and cook for 3 minutes, stirring constantly to stop it burning.

Remove from the heat and quickly stir in the egg yolk, strain if necessary, and let cool before serving with the sushi.

meat and poultry

Pickled plums (umeboshi) can be bought in Japanese and Asian supermarkets. They can be very salty and sharp, so you don't need too much. If you do not like the flavour of pickled plum, replace with pickled ginger.

sushi balls with roast pork and pickled plums

250 g pork fillet, in the piece

2 tablespoons Japanese soy sauce

1 tablespoon mirin (sweetened Japanese rice wine)

1 teaspoon Chinese hot pepper sauce or chilli sauce

½ recipe seasoned sushi rice (page 9)

10 Japanese pickled plums, halved and stoned

a roasting tin

makes 20

Put the pork in a plastic container. Mix the soy, mirin and hot pepper sauce in a bowl or jug, then pour over the pork. Set aside to marinate for 1 hour, turning the pork in the marinade every 15 minutes.

Put the pork in a roasting tin and pour the marinade over the top. Roast in a preheated oven to 200°C (400°F) Gas 6 for 15 minutes. Remove from the oven, let cool, then slice thinly – you should get about 20 slices.

Divide the rice into 20 balls. Take a piece of pickled plum and push it into the centre of a rice ball, then mould the rice around it so it is completely hidden. Repeat with the remaining plums and rice. Top each ball with a slice of roast pork.

Beef tataki is very rare marinated beef served in the sashimi style. If you do not like very rare beef, cook the fillet in a preheated oven at 180°C (350°F) Gas 4 for 10 minutes before returning to the frying pan to coat with sauce.

marinated beef sushi
(beef tataki)

2 teaspoons peanut oil

300 g beef eye fillet, in the piece

2 tablespoons Japanese soy sauce

2 tablespoons mirin (sweetened Japanese rice wine)

2 tablespoons rice vinegar

½ recipe seasoned sushi rice (page 9)

shredded pickled ginger, to serve (optional)

pickled red cabbage

175 g (about ⅛) red cabbage

100 g brown sugar

125 ml red wine vinegar

makes 18 sushi pieces, 250 ml pickled cabbage

To make the pickled red cabbage, finely slice the cabbage, removing any large core pieces, and chop into 3 cm lengths. Put in a medium saucepan, then add the brown sugar, vinegar and 4 tablespoons water. Bring to the boil, reduce the heat and simmer for 30 minutes.

Remove from the heat, let cool and store in a sealed container in the refrigerator for up to 1 week, or in the freezer for 3 months.

To prepare the beef, heat the oil in a frying pan and sear the beef on all sides until browned. Mix the soy sauce, mirin and vinegar in a bowl and pour over the beef, turning the beef to coat. Remove immediately from the heat and transfer the beef and its sauce to a dish. Let cool, cover and refrigerate for 1 hour, turning once.

Divide the rice into 18 balls, the size of a walnut, and shape into firm ovals.

Cut the beef in half lengthways (along the natural separation line), then slice as finely as possible. Wrap a piece of beef around the top of a rice ball and top with a little pickled cabbage or ginger.

miso soups

A good dashi, or soup stock, is the basis for any great miso soup. A very simple version requires only kombu and water, but fresh and dried fish give an exceptional result. Little dried fish are sold in packets in Japanese and other Asian supermarkets.

Many miso pastes come pre-mixed with dashi, but these recipes call for pure miso paste – so check the packet. If you do have dashi included in your paste, replace the dashi quantity with water. Different qualities of miso paste will have different strengths, so adjust quantities according to taste.

japanese dashi and combination miso soup

500 g fleshy fish bones

2 tablespoons dried fish or
1 tablespoon bonito flakes

5 cm piece of kombu

combination miso soup

2 tablespoons red miso paste

2 tablespoons white miso paste

**makes 1.5 litres dashi,
soup serves 4**

To make the dashi, put the fish bones, dried fish and kombu in a large stockpot, then add 3 litres water. Bring to the boil, reduce the heat and simmer, partially covered with a lid, for 2 hours, skimming any foam off the top from time to time. Strain and use immediately, or cool and store in the refrigerator for up to 2 days or freeze for up to 3 months.

To make the soup, put the red miso and white miso pastes in a small bowl. Add 4 tablespoons dashi and stir well.

Pour 1 litre dashi in a saucepan, bring to the boil, reduce to a simmer and stir in the miso mixture. Return to simmering point, but do not boil. Serve in 4 small bowls. (Reserve the remaining dashi for another use.)

The more mellow flavours of white miso make a perfect drink to serve with sushi rolls – the delicious and delicate taste of this soup will not overpower even the most subtle of sushi.

white miso soup
with wakame, tofu and lettuce

5 g wakame (dried seaweed)

1 litre dashi stock

4 tablespoons white miso paste

100 g silken tofu, cut into ½ cm cubes

¼ iceberg or other crisp lettuce, finely sliced (optional)

serves 4

Soak the wakame in a bowl of hot water for 15 minutes, then drain.

Pour the dashi stock into a saucepan, bring to the boil, then reduce to simmering. Mix the miso paste in a bowl with a few tablespoons of the dashi to loosen it, then stir it into the simmering stock. Add the tofu and wakame and cook in the soup for 1 minute.

Divide the lettuce, if using, between 4 bowls, ladle the hot soup over the top, then serve.

This heartier version of miso soup is perfect at the beginning or end of a sushi meal. Serve it before heavier meat- or poultry-based sushi rolls or after delicate fish or vegetarian rolls. It can also be beefed up with stir-fried vegetables as a great big bowl of soup for two.

red miso soup
with pork and noodles

200 g buckwheat noodles

1 litre dashi stock

1 small leek, finely sliced

3 tablespoons red miso paste

100 g roast pork, thinly sliced

serves 4

Fill a large saucepan three-quarters full of water and bring to the boil. Add the buckwheat noodles and return to the boil. Add 1 cup of cold water and bring to the boil again. Boil for 3 minutes, drain, rinse in cold water and drain again.

Pour the dashi stock into a saucepan and bring to the boil. Add the leeks and reduce to a simmer. Mix the miso paste in a bowl with a few tablespoons of the dashi to loosen it, then stir it into the simmering stock.

Divide the noodles and slices of roast pork between 4 bowls, ladle over the hot soup, then serve.

You need only about one-third of this batter for this recipe, but half an egg seems difficult to work with, so use the rest of the batter for tempura vegetables or prawns. Alternatively, you could use the pressed croutons sold in Japanese stores.

red miso soup
with spring onions and tempura croutons

1 litre dashi stock

3 tablespoons red miso paste

2 spring onions, finely sliced

tempura croutons

1 egg, separated

1 tablespoon lemon juice

150 ml iced water

60 g plain flour

peanut or safflower oil, for frying

serves 4

To make the batter, put the egg yolk, lemon juice and iced water in a bowl. Whisk gently, then whisk in the flour to form a smooth batter. Do not overmix.

Whisk the egg white in a second bowl until stiff but not dry, then fold into the batter.

To cook the croutons, fill a large wok or saucepan one-third full with oil and heat to 190°C (375°F), or until a small cube of bread turns golden in 30 seconds.

Carefully drop teaspoons of the batter into the oil and cook for 30 seconds until crispy. Scoop out and drain on kitchen paper.

Pour the dashi into a saucepan, bring to the boil, then reduce to a simmer. Mix the miso paste with a few tablespoons of the dashi to loosen it, then stir it into the simmering stock. Divide the stock between 4 bowls, add the croutons and spring onions and serve.

pickled ginger

150 g piece of fresh ginger

1 tablespoon salt

125 ml rice vinegar

115 g sugar

1 slice fresh beetroot, 1 red radish, sliced, or a drop of red food colouring (optional)

makes about 250 ml

Peel the ginger and slice it very finely with a mandoline or vegetable peeler. Put it in a large sieve or colander and sprinkle with salt. Set aside for 30 minutes, then rinse thoroughly.

Put the rice vinegar and sugar in a saucepan, add 60 ml water and bring to the boil, stirring until the sugar has dissolved. Boil for 5 minutes. Let cool, then pour over the ginger. If you would like it to be pink, like shop-bought ginger, add the beetroot, radish or food colouring. Cover and refrigerate for at least 24 hours or until needed.

Pickled ginger is the traditional companion for sushi. The subtle flavouring of raw fish, delicate rice and fresh vegetables can easily be overpowered by the lingering flavours of previous morsels. Ginger helps cleanse the palate, introducing a sharp freshness that stimulates the taste buds for the next delight.

accompaniments

mixed pickles

Other vegetables can be pickled and served with sushi alongside ginger. They look wonderfully colourful, adding a touch of drama to your sushi platter and making it appear very professional.

½ cucumber, about 10 cm long

1 carrot, about 100 g

100 g daikon radish, peeled, or 6 red radishes

¼ small green cabbage, about 150 g

6 garlic cloves, finely sliced

1 tablespoon salt

½ lemon, sliced

250 ml rice vinegar

175 g sugar

makes about 500 ml

Cut the cucumber in half lengthways and scoop out the seeds. Slice the cucumber, carrot and radish into very thin strips.

Slice the cabbage into 1 cm strips. Put all the vegetables and garlic in a colander, sprinkle with salt and toss well. Set aside for 30 minutes, then rinse thoroughly and top with the sliced lemon.

Put the rice vinegar and sugar in a saucepan with 60 ml water. Bring to the boil, stirring until the sugar has dissolved. Boil for 5 minutes. Let cool, then pour over the vegetables and lemon. Cover and refrigerate for at least 24 hours or until needed. Keeps for 1 month in the refrigerator.

wasabi paste

Most of the wasabi we buy in tubes is a mixture of horseradish and wasabi – or it can be just horseradish dyed green. If you buy wasabi paste from a Japanese market, you will have a selection of various qualities, and it is always preferable to buy the best.

Many Japanese cooks prefer to mix their own paste from silver-grey wasabi powder, sold in small cans, like paprika, believing that the flavour is stronger and sharper.

The fresh roots are not widely available, even in Japan, but if you see them in a specialist greengrocer, sold on a bed of ice, do try them. To experience the real flavour and rush of wasabi you can make your own paste from them. Traditionally grated using a sharkskin grater, a porcelain ginger grater or a very fine abrasive zester will also work. After grating, the heat in wasabi lasts for only about 10 minutes, so you must use it straight away.

wasabi from powder

1 teaspoon wasabi powder

serves 1

Put the wasabi powder in a small bowl, such as an eggcup. Add 1 teaspoon water and mix with the end of a chopstick. Serve immediately.

fresh wasabi paste

1 fresh wasabi root

a wasabi grater or ginger grater

serves 6–8

Scrape or peel off the rough skin from the root. Using a circular motion, rub the wasabi gently against an abrasive grater onto a chopping board. Pound and chop the grated wasabi to a fine paste with a large knife or cleaver. Consume within 10 minutes.

Note To keep the wasabi from discolouring for as long as possible, turn the little bowl upside down until serving – this will stop the air getting at it.

index